For my brother, Loïc.

Published 1986
by Merehurst Press
5, Great James Street
London WC1N 3DA
by arrangement
with Temps de Pose Editions
38, rue de la République
27500 Pont-Audemer. France
© Copyright 1986 photographs: Stéphane DUROY
© Copyright 1986 text: Philippe GANIER RAYMOND

ISBN 0-948075-49-X

Layout: Corinne REYMOND
Photocomposition: Graphelec Paris
Printed in Italy by SAGDOS Brugherio-Milano
Translated by Veronica HAMMOND

2

BERLIN

Photographs
Stéphane DUROY

Text
Philippe GANIER RAYMOND

MEREHURST PRESS
— LONDON —

The Wall of Shame.

East Berlin considers this harshly illuminated no-man's-land as the "anti-fascist bulwark".

A doting father.

The Kneipe - the pub - a second home.

Cabaret.

Entertainers and drag shows continue the tradition of the Berlin music hall; here at the Dhollywood.

The S-Bahn, key to Berlin.

The second world war reduced Berlin to nothing and on the thirteenth of August 1961 this void was cut in two by a grey wall, now painted white so that at night fugitives are clearly silhouetted in the floodlights.

Berlin could have been the capital of human suffering, the Mecca of despair. Nothing is further from the truth. Today Berlin is the European capital of the theatre. Such an apt setting for tragedy can but inspire superb dramas or icy comedies. I am thinking of the Botho Strauss plays that Peter Stein directs at the Schaubühne and of the plays put on in East Berlin by Ekkehart Schall, who has taken up the Brechtian torch with an unfaltering hand at the Schiffbauerdamm theatre.

But the theatre is in the street too and more especially in the "Kneipe" and the Berlin cafés (Berlin boasts more cafés and pubs per square mile than any other place in the world).

People from Moabit, Wannsee and Wedding come here to gossip, in public and in loud voices, with the first stranger they meet. Sometimes you feel, both East Berlin and West Berlin is the sum of the loneliness of five million individuals. The wall is not responsible. (Read "Berliner Alexander Platz" by Alfred Doblin). After the war, the destruction, after the rebuilding, folkhero, Franz Biberkopf is still alive, a wandering, tragically naïve, slang-talking character.

This theatre has its musical accompaniment. It runs on rails, those of the S-Bahn, the elevated urban railway. It is the "Clang of Berlin" — the sound of Berlin. A sort of railway tango, gloomy and plaintive in the background, a rhythmical beat against which people's lives are unconsciously lived out. Uwe Johnson is a great German writer, unknown outside Germany. He died recently, not far from London. He has written a marvellous book: "Berliner Sachen", Items from Berlin. It is the libretto, one might say, of an opera set on the wharfs of the Spree river and the Landwehrkanal.

Johnson describes this metronomic pulse which fills the nights and blurs conversations. The S-Bahn is the key to Berlin. Each station, with its little wobbling cobblestones, its closed-down cafés, its signs clattering in the wind and its long-haired, red-capped inspectors, represents the silent essence of what is Berlin. The blustering wind makes the birch trees rustle.

*Gesundbrunnen,
the famous S-Bahn station
from which there have been
spectacular escapes.*

The best way to survey the city is from the elevated railway. It clatters over Wedding (formerly Red Wedding), over peaceful Steglitz, over self-conscious Charlottenbourg and on from Staaken, ending its journey at Friedrichstrasse, the walled-up station: the gate to East Berlin. The armoured plated-glass door lets through in the same throng the foreigner, curious and unconcerned, and the old German, silent and distressed.

It is common knowledge that East Berlin women over sixty years old may go and see their relations who live in West Berlin.

I witnessed the following scene one day. A woman was coming back to the East side with a doll, for her grand-daughter, presumably. The customs officer seized it and took it to pieces; both arms came off, both legs. Then the head. And he spread the dismembered plastic form on the counter. Since the inside of the doll was empty he allowed the old lady through. But she stood there, alone, and screwed the limbs back on. And the head. I shall never forget the movement of her hands and that frozen despair which showed in her. An incident which demonstrates silently and perhaps, therefore, more forcibly the Berliners's predicament than the daily border skirmishes.

Berlin has been walled off, surrounded by a concrete arc with a circumference of hundred and two miles, with pockets of land enclosed in the north, and in the south. The handful of people residing in these "pockets" have to ring the bell at the armour-plated sliding-doors in order to get home. Everyday-life has been skilfully shaped into silent tragedy with consummate craft, applied to the most monstrous architectural artefact in the history of mankind: there is no precedent for the Berlin wall. The great Wall of China is in no way analogous. Its purpose was to defend the region from the Mongols' invasion. The 1961 Wall is the first example of a domestic bulwark. An unique case of state schizophrenia.

People claim they can find a precedent. They talk of the tower of Kant and that of Hölderlin. Of a specific German atavism, of an obsessive desire for impassable barriers, of a deep unconscious yearning for the tangible frontiers that nature has denied Germany. That is an appalling over-simplification. Such people sparked off the first post-war anti-communist insurrection in East Berlin in 1953. After that came Poznan and then Budapest. Berliners dislike barriers even if they can build admirable barricades, but they are also obsessed with a feeling of guilt. I beleive that the Wall is considered by many Berliners as a well-deserved punishment. And since this is a material vision of eternity, West Berliners accept the wall with a sort of spellbound ecstasy. Berlin is a city of antitheses.

Deserted and dismal, Potsdamer Square, formerly the liveliest square in Europe is now nothing but a stopping-place on the tourist circuit.

Potsdamer Platz 1929

*Because of the changing political situation,
the S-Bahn has been superseded
as a means of transport
in West Berlin.*

A chilly dawn in Kreuzberg...

at Wedding.

The changing face of Berlin.

A picture of the S-Bahn which already belongs to the past.

In the shadow of the Wall.

There are fifty thousand allotments, a favourite German leisure activity, close to the Wall, as in the Bornholmer Strasse here.

*A former battlefield
has become a playground.*

A symbol of the division of Berlin.

In front of the Brandenburg Gate a group of British tanks guards the Soviet war memorial.

Bric-à-brac:
traces of the upheavals
of history.

Nº 18, Grossbeeren Strasse.

*The November light
casts a warm glow
on this romantic building.*

People in Kreuzberg,
an area of intense
creative activity.

Café Einstein: unchanging in a city of constant change.

Berlin can be, depending on the observer, the end of the world served up with a smile in a fast-food restaurant. A state of permanent revolt or of lethargy. Surprisingly Berlin is not an aggressive city, it is easy to confuse policemen with park attendants. Berlin is a city both somnolent and effervescent which retires to bed late, stretching its limbs in a cacaphony of metalic sounds. Bewildered Allied troops on leave wander in the many open spaces which exist within the walled city.

Nothing here has any affinity with Prussian rigidity. As soon as your back is turned the city alters, re-models itself. Berlin is a mutant. The pace is hectic. People are appointed to new positions daily. One day a café is open, the next it has closed down. In Berlin buildings are torn apart, demolished and re-built like lightning. Which is strange when you consider that Berliners are thought of as the only examples of indolent Germans.

There is however one place which does not change: the Einstein Café in Kurfürstenstrasse. It is on the first floor, but has a shaded garden. In one of the rooms a large Bechstein of the Thirties lies under dustsheets waiting for someone to bring to life its dormant keys, all yellow and worn like a smoker's teeth. The Einstein café is one of the landmarks of Berlin. "Everyone" was, and is to be found there. From Günter Grass to Wim Wenders, from Nina Hagen to the marvellous writer Hans-Joachim Schaedlich. Surprisingly, the owner is from Vienna. An immigrant weary of the haughtiness of this narcissistic town. A string-quartet plays impertinently out of tune.

And then there is the "Metropole" where many a German show business career has taken form. Just opposite, there is the flea market, which has spread over a disused underground station. Go there Saturday morning at eleven-thirty in time for Frühschoppen-a solid breakfast-cum-elevenses. It is full of local colour, and it is one of the places where Berliners are the most "authentic", where you can listen, until your head spins, to those long-winded sentences filled with many jokey asides and references, some of them uninspired but none of them without some amusement value. After that you must go to the zoo, the best in Europe and the most humane.

Kreuzberg, a traditionally working-class area inhabited by cultural and ethnic minorities.

Berlin was nothing a hundred and fifty years ago. Just a cattle market on marshy ground. The capital of Prussia was Potsdam. French Hugenots gave this village an urban structure. One day Berlin gave itself an opera house; the two Guillaume, the First and the Second, made Berlin into a military capital, something that went right against the grain of Berliners who are pseudo-Prussians and staunch libertarians. Rosa Luxembourg was a great woman but she was totally wrong when she declared: "Berliners will never start a Revolution. They would have to walk on the grass". She may be forgiven since she came from Silesia ! Rosa Luxembourg was assassinated in 1919 on the spot where the Europa centre now stands. A martyr for her cause.

Is Berlin a city in D minor? The key of tragedy; the perfect paroxysmal chord. To obtain tickets for one of the concerts given by the Berlin Philharmonic Orchestra, people sleep out in the Tiergarten for several days and nights running. One cannot talk of Berlin without transmitting the echo of its music. Whether it be Rock, universally present, or classical music, audiences are gravely attentive.

Berlin is a city where the appointment of a new clarinettist to the Philharmonic is a momentous event, enthusiastically debated in the newspapers and the pubs. In the same vein, every German creative artist, whether he be a painter, a musician or a writer has to serve an apprenticeship in the former capital. It is here that creativity blossoms, that criticism and pertinent judgements flourish. It is also a city that dulls the senses, without one's realizing. It is always necessary to get away to take an objective view, Günter Grass did this as did many others.

Distress.

That Berlin may live on.

At the Jerusalem cemetery, the faces on the tombs are the work of Kurt Mühlenhampt, a Berlin primitive artist.

*Day after day
they stare
at the Wall.*

*Old and dilapidated buildings
are being replaced
by modern blocks
all over Berlin.*

Illusion.

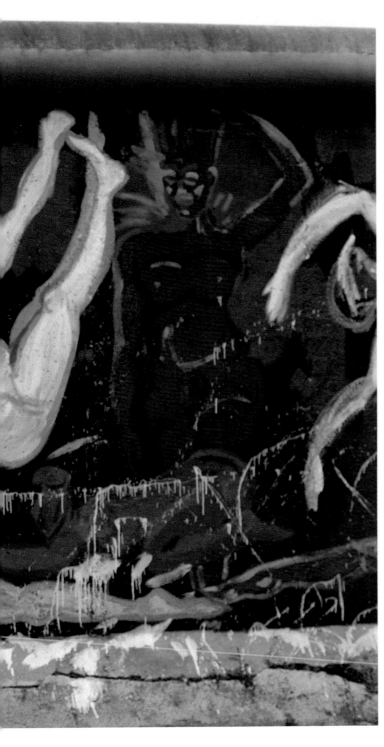

*By covering the Wall
with graffiti
foreigners fondly imagine
they are improving
the look of Berlin.*

An early morning meeting.

A place where people meet with their dogs.

*In East Berlin, whose
flourishing black market
attracts many West Berliners,
capitalist pensions represent
a comfortable income.*

Work on the West side,
spend on the East side.

Alleyways, courtyards and demolition sites provide a wealth of play-areas.

Laughing Turkish children
at play in Kreuzberg.

Incessant re-building.

Years after the war, Berlin still looks like a bomb site.

A drizzling November evening.

*The nerve centre
for the occupying
forces' intelligence services.*

Expressionless,
this woman ignores
the slogan of the R.A.F.
- Red Army Faction -
the military wing
of the Baader-Meinhof group.

Berlin: heart of the world.

Every one will tell you: the centre of Berlin is the Kurfüstendamm which at night looks like an immense flaming cross. Ku Damm, with its adjoining streets, Knesebeckstrasse, Kantstrasse, Fasanenstrasse... There is also, dozing in the shade of its lime and jasmine trees; Friedenau, the provincial town, and Kreuzberg and Wedding where the immigrant Turks and native Berliners live together (a situation which would be a tinderbox anywhere else) in almost perfect amity; is not each of these mutually exclusive areas, which taken together form Berlin, in fact the heart of Berlin?

Berlin is a city in perpetual motion. One week Kantstrasse is the place to see and to be seen, the next one must be at Wannsee, by the water. Some people will say that the Bistroquet is no longer the in-place and that you must go along to the Florian café on Savigny Platz. Savigny Platz is perhaps the only constant in the fashionable areas of Berlin. You get off the S-Bahn. On your left there is a railway bridge on which, surely you remember? Lisa Minnelli cries in "Cabaret".

This is where the Reste Fidèle (remain faithful) road begins. If Berlin can boast one street which epitomizes the whole city, this is the one. Drug centre of Berlin, if Berlin loses its soul and dies it will be because of the far-reaching effects of the activity here. One sees elegantly turned-out parents, zig-zagging between the hooligans and the pimps as they take their children to the local school. Sunday morning is devoted to the Frühschoppen, the Berliners' brunch, washed down with beer or hock and sometimes over a game of chess. People relate what happened the night before-a night full of complications and perils, like all Berlin nights. Savigny Platz and Bleibtreustrasse is an avenue lined with lime trees instead of birch. There are four cafés, the last of which, near the Ku Damm is called "Reste Fidèle" written in French. You are unquestioningly accepted provided you are a good listener.

Savigny Platz is a treasure trove. Stars from the neighbouring peep-show come and discuss the changing face of Berlin with architects in a café. At the Florian café Kristo's collaborators are preparing the final details of his latest work, the wrapping up of Pont Neuf in Paris. Wim Wenders stops by from his native Kreuzberg and outlines the plot of a film that he would like to shoot in Pondichery. Day gives way to night unremarked.

A cheerless daily life looks down on escapist advertising.

Berlin, a city full of food and drink.

Berlin, an open-air city.

People are drinking scandalously adulterated French wines, the chairs are wobbly and the stories incredibly complicated.

You ask : "But why did you choose Berlin?" Someone answers: "Because", (as the French writer, Boris Vian, translating Brecht, would say)"Here everything works jolly well".

A few yards away, the Springer gallery looks like a rectangular eye. At certain times a pale indigo light glows from the shop. The Springer gallery is an admirable testimony to the permanence of Berlin, spanning the ruins. At Springer's you can find, from month to month Expressionist paintings, works from "Die Brücke" school, once in a while a Grosz or an Otto Dix, even an Emil Nolde but also painters who are not yet well-known in Germany but will not remain so for long. One day Springer is asked whether it would not be a good idea to ask modern artists to decorate the Wall. He answers, aghast: "Works of death cannot be decorated".

Sweets...
for the sweet.

A night scene.

Dschungel, the exclusive evening haunt of the Berlin intelligentsia.

*Music lovers at
the Einstein café.*

*One of the few remaining
working-class cafés
with its snooker table.*

Werner Gädke,
the all-knowing
Head Porter.

*Afternoon tea
in a pre-war
setting.*

Nostalgia.

The Sixties rock and roll at the Excess café.

*More cafés
than anywhere else
in the world.*

In the depth of the night.

*Pulsating Berlin
where the pace of life
is perpetually crazy.*

Building the future.

During the last war ninety per cent of all buildings were destroyed or damaged.
East Berlin continues to buy the rubble.

The most expensive wall in the world.

Its erection cost the staggering sum of twenty million marks.

Berlin: dreams and cynicism.

Berlin, without a blueprint, has succeeded in creating something that every applied ideology has failed to achieve: a classless society. One thinks of Plato, who laboured to construct an ideal city and only drew up the draft for all future totalitarian societies. Here it just happened. After the absolutist horror, Germany or committing the most spectacular cultural suicide in modern history by burning its books and killing its Jews, the country itself had to work out a sphere of freedom and tolerance. Such a gesture springs from an inexplicable collective instinct. But at the heart of the matter is a paradox that all this became possible with the building of the Berlin Wall.

When Walter Ulbricht finally managed to persuade Krushchev that the Wall was essential, the man from Saxony with the goatee beard and the high-pitched girlish or voice did not realize that he was laying the foundations in West Berlin of the most important cultural centre in Europe. Obviously the absurd and the tragic attract artists as flypaper attracts flies... The paradox is only skin-deep.

Let no one forget how many deaths the wall has caused in twenty five years. There have been, there always will be, hair-raisingly successful escapes,but how many fugitives have been killed in the process since 1961? Exact figures are unobtainable and obviously this is not a common subject of conversation in West Berlin. Moreover, on the other side in the G.D.R., from motives of caution rather than indifference, no one mentions the subject either. But recently, while East Berlin was celebrating the twenty fifth anniversary of the building of the "anti-fascist bulwark", the G.D.R. police undertook the razing of the buildings, or what remained of them, on the ill-fated Bernauerstrasse in order to replace them with a white wall. Just previously (symbolic action!) the Church of Reconciliation, situated in no-man's-land, had been blown up. History is being sedulously obliterated whilst ostensibly commemorating it.

In Berlin, a city which presents one of the most incredible legal imbroglios in international law (four zones of occupation; plus the capital of an independant state, the German Democratic Republic; plus a West German municipal council, which is not however part of the Federal Republic; plus a local police force which safeguards the English, who protect the Russian soldiers guarding the Red Army memorial and so on...) anything and everything is possible. Dreams and nightmares.

Night and day,
ten thousand soldiers
guard the Wall.

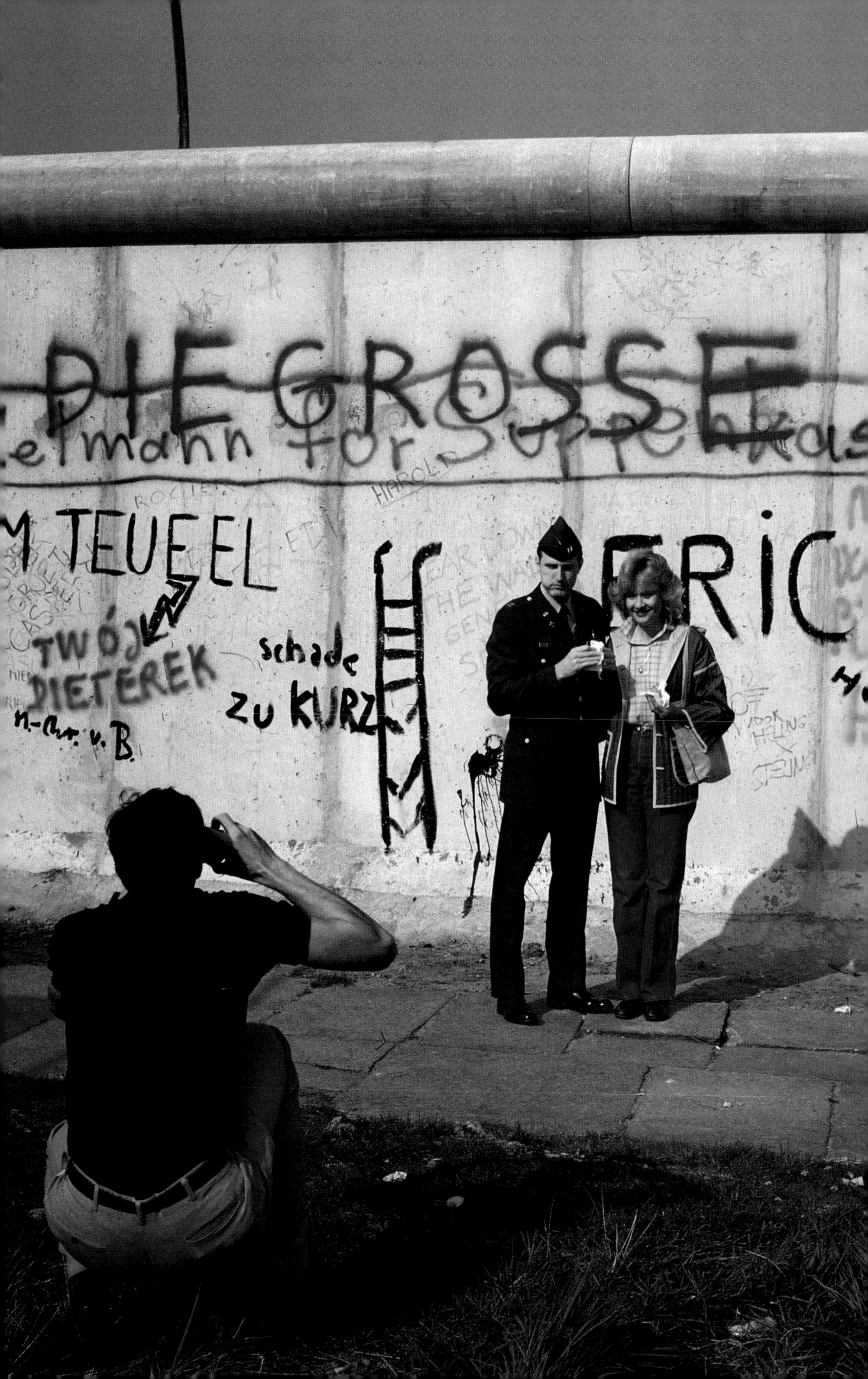
DIE GROSSE
HAROLD
ERIC
TWÓJ
DIETEREK
schade
zu KURZ

*For tourists from West Berlin
or "vopos" (Soviet soldiers) from East Berlin,
the Wall is always the background
for a commemorative photograph.*

Schönewalde, Heiligensee, Glienicke, Prenzlauerberg... These names of areas of Berlin are like the lines of a poem that one recites while the trams whine along Chaussee Strasse and Dimitroff Straff on the oder side of the Wall. Way over there, at Spandau, the life of Rudolf Hess, the last prisoner left after Nüremberg, is winding to its close. A human pea in a mattress of bricks. Here history has not been obliterated. It is being mummified. Hess stands as a testimony that we cannot ignore all that has passed. He also provides a heavensent pretext for the Western Allies and the Russians to render one another military honours once a week. The prison will probably be demolished and salutes merely exchanged at Checkpoint Charlie.

The secret of the liberty of Berlin is that history passed it by. History marches on but elsewhere.

*Bernauer Strasse,
the saddest street
in the world,
on the thirteenth
of August 1961...*

*...The houses are being
bricked up.
To get away,
people jump out
of their windows.*

The toll of the last war:
120, 000 deaths,
6, 000 suicides
and 20, 000 rapes.

No entry for German nationals.

Checkpoint Charlie,
a landmark in the legend
which has built up
around the Wall,
is the border passage
for foreigners and
for the personnel belonging
to the occupying forces.

The walls cry...

...and dance.

Relaxing in West Berlin.

An improvised terrace adjoining the Wall.

*The biggest
exhibition space
in the world:
103 miles long.*

Death in its starkness.

"No future":
the punk slogan.

Dancing the "Pogo".

The "Pogo", a frenzied violent dance, is the punk expression of life.

A pavement holiday.

*Squatters sunbathe
on matresses and
old car seats.*

Metropolis.

*Berlin accepts
any and every form
of eccentricity.*

Creation.

For Heidi Barthelemie, West Berlin remains the paradise of the arts world.

*Bertholt Brecht
at the Des Western theatre.*

Dschungel,
the famous disco-bar.

*An incident at
Checkpoint Charlie.
Refugees burn
the G.D.R. flag
in full view
of the "vopos".
East and West Berlin
face to face
along the Wall.*

At Penny Lane's:
the hair stylist.

Multi-faceted Berlin.

*The Kuckuck wall,
formerly the headquarters
of the Berlin Alternative
Art Group.*

Bebop.

*Bebop live at
the Metropolis.*

The Reichstag.

The building was set on fire in 1933; the Nazis accused the Communists and took reprisal against them.

Albert Merz.

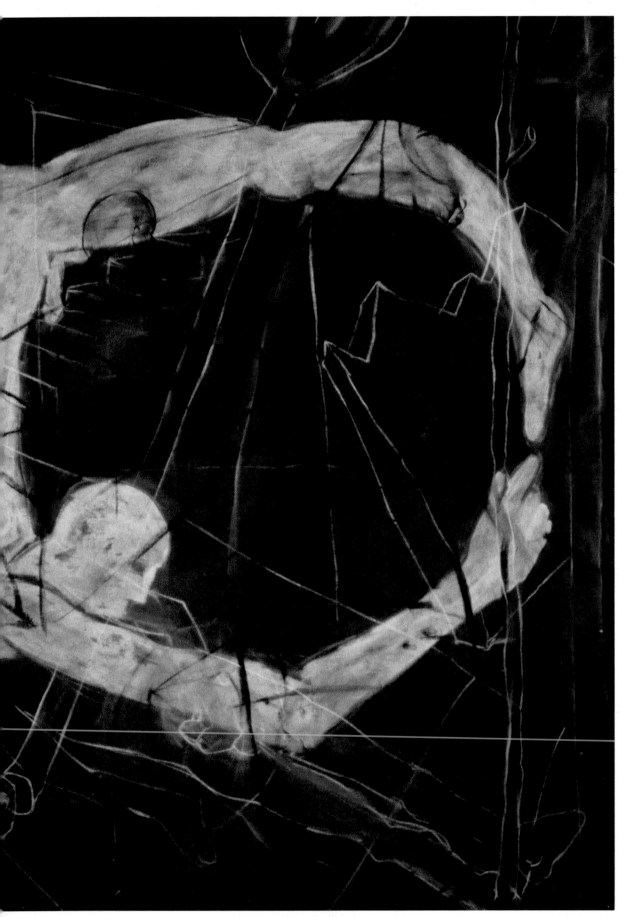

Albert Merz, a Swiss-born painter, finds his inspiration in Berlin.

ACKNOWLEDGEMENTS

Stéphane Duroy
and Temps de Pose Editions
would particularly like
to thank the following:

In West Germany:

Mme Evelyn Holst
Mme Marie-Louise Von Plessen
Mme Ruth Eichhorn
M. Wolfgang Behnken
Stern Magazine

In Great Britain:

M. Hendrik Vollers
M. Eddie Girardet
The Photographers' Gallery

In France:

Melle Corinne Reymond
Mme Dorothée Selz
Mme Barbara Grosset
M. Philippe Ganier Raymond
M. Remi Berli
Mme Nicole Donnat
Air France

Goossens

For their contribution
to the production of this book.